'Alors, je te laisse … on dirait que French actor Rose affectionate together at the ca was still falling on the bo away re

h som oppos him her sto indi ent projected Doll's Hou performances Albi for another young actors and borrowed two th Paul; Marcel had a a fortnight on four was impossible. T to Paris and as sh them, She would have

Soie ville avec the fat e tapped left them rain ps ds se

d a g ft wetting nylon

sly g the Builder, The end after only six open their week at mpany of earnest nded. Rose had the leading actor wo, but to live for get herself to Albi g back th all of money. nd when the rain

LOVE CHANGES EVERYTHING

Love,
love changes everything:
hands and faces,
earth and sky.
Love,
love changes everything:
how you live and
how you die.

Love
can make the summer fly
or a night
seem like a lifetime.

Yes, love,
love changes everything:
now I tremble
at your name.
Nothing in the
world will ever
be the same.

Love,
love changes everything:
days are longer,
words mean more.
Love,
love changes everything:
pain is deeper
than before.

Love will turn your world around,
and that world
will last for ever.

Yes, love,
love changes everything,
brings you glory,
brings you shame.
Nothing in the
world will ever
be the same.

Off
into the world we go,
planning futures,
shaping years.
Love
bursts in, and suddenly
all our wisdom
disappears.

Love makes fools of everyone:
all the rules
we make are broken.

Yes, love,
love changes everyone.
Live or perish
in its flame.
Love will never,
never let you
be the same.

PARLEZ-VOUS FRANÇAIS?

'Well, Mademo[...]vered most of the questions I came [...] speaking for the first ti[...] Englis[...]

[...] old J[...] Alexis, still in the same [...]

[...] old [...] y worried . . . so I thought out of co[...] come down and put things straight[...]

'I have a lot to [...] you are here there [...]

Parlez-vous français?
Je suis sad.
Parlez-vous français?
I feel bad.

How do you say
"ce soir vous êtes
si belle"?

I only know
a word or so,
like "cat" and "school" –
je suis fool.

Parlez-vous français?
Please say "oui".
Parlez-vous français?
Speak to me.

Alexis reappear[...]sses and hugging bottles.

'Chambéry verr[...] *porto?*' he asked.

'*Porto* is what Ro[...]

'Chambéry [...]ss and gave it to him and filled a gl[...]e for himself.

'Now, my dear [...] it all started,' his uncle asked him[...]g tone and then suddenly added: [...]nt any misunder-standi[...]—I ough[...]ooked a room for myself at [...]Hôte[...]nt to be *de trop*. I shall take myself o[...]

How do you say,
"vous êtes jolie,
mam'selle"?

Chérie,
where do I commencer,
if you won't parler français
with me?

Parlez-vous français?
Say you do!
Parlez-vous français?
Tell me true!

How do you say
"Je suis unhappy
fella"?

Chérie,
adieu to drinks and danser,
if you won't parler français
with me.

Unless you say "oui" . . .
adieu to drinks and danser
if you won't parler français
with me.

SEEING IS BELIEVING

Seeing is believing,
and in my arms I see her:
she's here,
really here,
really mine now –
she seems at home here . . .

Seeing is believing.
I dreamt that it would be her:
at last
life is full,
life is fine now . . .

Whatever happens,
one thing is certain:
each time I see
a train go by,
I'll think of us,
the night, the sky
forever . . .

*He's young,
very young,
but appealing –
I feel I know him . . .*

*Seeing is believing,
and I like what I see here.
I like
where I am,
what I'm feeling . . .*

'Damn him for ...
said to himself b...
Rose had brough...
latter had n... had...
Next ...
unclou... weath...
moments passion...
laughing at Alexis...
the twinkling of a...
and declare that A...
her fault. She was ...

Alexis could n...
made up his mi...
unendurabl...
Rose disapp...
becoming a...
town to go t...

Next mo...
while she w...

'Get up; w...

'What do... sitting bolt
upright.

'We are ta...

'See the P... y well out of
the window...

'You are ... a horse.'

'When ... ter?'

'Yesterd... imaginative
boy.'

'Darling, ... goodness ...

What are we doing?
Can you believe it?
A starving actress and
a star-struck boy –
oh well, I might
as well enjoy
the moment . . .

Whatever happens,
we have this moment.
Who needs tomorrow,
when we have today?
Tonight we'll mean
the things we say
forever.

Seeing is believing!
My life is just beginning!
We touched,
and my head won't stop spinning
from winning
your love!

...ne. Rose was at
...ddenly burst out
...ing him. Then, in
...erself on the head
...t was all
...character.
...essed her, b... he
...h day would be
...e afternoon
...when he was
...een into the
...urly coffee

...yrenees.'

CHANSON D'ENFANCE

Pas de tendresse
et pas de joie,
loin d'ici,
loin de toi.

Rien de plus triste
que mes soupirs,
lorsque vient le jour
où il me faut partir.

Chanson d'enfance,
tu vis toujours dans mon coeur.
Toi, la plus douce!
Toi, la plus tendre!

OTHER PLEASURES

Other pleasures,
and I've known many . . .
Afternoons
in warm Venetian squares,
brief encounters,
long siestas . . .
Pleasures old and new
can't compare with you.

You amaze me!
Where did you come from?
You do things
champagne could never do.
Crystal winters,
crimson summers . . .
Other pleasures –
I would trade them all
for you.

Pleasures old and new
can't compare with you . . .

Wild mimosa,
the scent of evening,
shuttered rooms
with sunlight breaking through,
crazy soirées,
lazy Sundays . . .
Other pleasures –
I would trade them all
for you.

Sailing off
in the night
on a silver lake . . .
Taking more
from this life
than I ought to take . . .
Other pleasures –
I would trade them all
for you.

to have lunch wi[...]taurant. It would
have been a pleas[...] relationship, but
Alexis said he ha[...]
would be ridiculo[...]
the hope that Ro[...]
an end between th[...]
to renew relations[...]
so. Yet he knew [...]
afternoon and th[...]
would be out of [...]
her. Why, he aske[...]
uncertainty, this t[...]on?
Alexis had er[...] with women and
friendships with t[...] seen Rose, but he
had not felt for a[...] e agitation which

MERMAID SONG

I am a mermaid
with golden hair . . .
I've never seen one like you!

Not all us mermaids
have silver tails –
I have no tail at all.

*Well I've never
seen any mermaids
with knobbly knees!
I'd say this tale
was a touch too tall,
maybe a touch too tall.*

Sailors would smash on
my jagged rock,
lured by my siren's song.

*It isn't the
song of the siren
that tortures men –
that's where your theory
goes sadly wrong,
that's where it all goes wrong.*

I thought you'd know better.
You know nothing
about mermaids.

a dirty hall wi[...]ury staircase into
which a ramshack[...]serted. Alexis was
in a state of[...]doing at last what
six years before [...]mpted to do but
which, when the [...]ed, he had always

*You know nothing
about sailors.*
I do!
much more than you!
If you were a sailor
and heard my song,
would you be lured by me?

*I wouldn't be
foolish enough to
go near your rock –
I'd steer my galleon out to sea . . .
lonely and lost at sea . . .*

THE FIRST MAN YOU REMEMBER

bedroom. It was ... ould not find the switch.

Next moment ... ge bedroom ...thrown open and ... naked ... a ... caught over the ...'s naked limbs as ...ut ... h h... exis went in and, ...hel... his a... Alexis. 'But I don't ...uch ... per... beautiful with a strand of her lon... one eye. Though completely occup... ether there was a spark of life left, A... ir in Rose's tawny fleece. He had nev... e. She had picked up the quilt from ... round her body under the a... ong, so that her powerful shoulder...

She watched w... Alexis broke the capsule under Sir C...

'There's no pul... k he is breathing. Give me your mirr...

Rose picked u... watched silent... while Alexis held i...

'I suppo... re... would b... body ov...

'I can ... to him.

I want to be
the first man you remember,
I want to be
the last man you forget.
I want to be
the one you always turn to,
I want to be
the one you won't regret.

May I be first
to say you look delightful?
May I be first
to dance you round the floor?
The very first
to see your face by moonlight?
The very first
to walk you to your door?

Well young man, I'd be delighted!
There is nothing I would rather do!
What could be a sweeter memory
than sharing my first dance with you?

I want to be
the first man you remember . . .
The very first
to sweep me off my feet.
I want to be
the one you always turn to . . .
The first to make
my young heart miss a beat.

Seems the stars are far below us.
The moon has never felt like this before.
Our first dance will be forever.
And may it lead to many more.

I want to be
the first man you remember . . .
The very first
to sweep me off my feet.
I want to be
the one you always turn to . . .
The first to make
your young heart miss a beat.

The very first . . .
The very first . . .

HAND ME THE WINE AND THE DICE

George was an original man.
He did not want to change human life.
He rejoiced in the way we are made.
He did not look forward to heaven –
he was happy with the earth.
He loved and understood
the flesh, food, wine, love . . .
He lived for today and firmly believed:

poem about the ⟨...⟩ the last lines of
which I shall rea⟨...⟩ thinking of that
poem that led hir⟨...⟩ friends. I
shall read it in ⟨...⟩slation, for the
majority of you h⟨...⟩

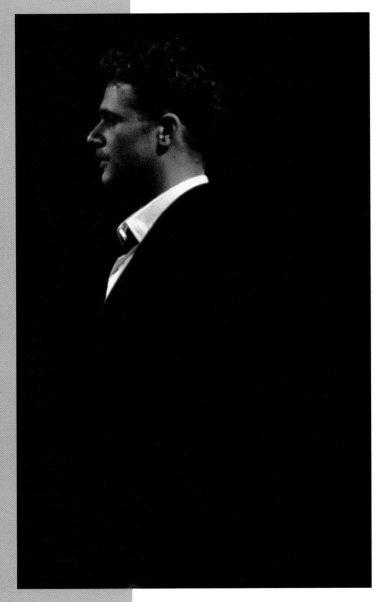

lover of poetry an⟨...⟩

Without more ⟨...⟩ a translation of
Giulietta's speech⟨...⟩mmitted to heart.
When he had finis⟨...⟩ own.
His words were ⟨...⟩ct simplicity; he
seemed to be sp⟨...⟩ every word was

If death were given a voice,
that voice would scream through the sky:
live while you may, for I am coming . . .

So . . .

Hand me the wine and the dice,
I want my carnival now,
while I have thirst and lust for living!
So gather all you can reap,
before you're under the plough –
the hand of death is unforgiving!

Alexis half-fille[...] [...]e barrel and then
they walked [...] where he had left
his car. It was [...]ouse and nobody
could see them dr[...]

When Alexis rang [...] [...]y on
the following day [...] She said
nothing and did [...]nd Vincent were
sitting at the bre[...]g-gowns. Marcel
was there too.

'I came to tak[...] and find you still
having [...]

Ro[...]ed a[...] [...]s a
change in her.

'Have a glass [...] just
getting to that stag[...]

'I'll be ready i[...] the
room.

'What have yo[...] [...]sked
Rose.

'Nothing so fa[...] r the
mulberry [...] room
where s[...]

Vincen[...]

'*Trincquet,* he [...]

'Well, I'm wor[...] [...]at's a
fact,' said Ros[...]

'I don'[...] [...]tuation
in my o[...]

'You ma[...]

Hand me the wine and the dice,
while there are grapes on the vine –
life is a round of endless pleasures!
The end is always in sight,
but it tastes better with wine –
why pour your life in tiny measures?

Hand me the wine and the dice,
the time is racing away –
there's not a taste that's not worth trying!
And if tomorrow it ends,
I won't have wasted today –
I will have lived when I am dying!

Hand me the wine and the dice,
I want my carnival now,
while I have thirst and lust for living!
So gather all you can reap,
before you're under the plough –
life is a round
of flesh, food, wine, love . . .

ANYTHING BUT LONELY

Anything but lonely,
anything but empty rooms.
There's so much in life to share –
what's the sense when no-one else is there?

Anything but lonely,
anything but only me.
Quiet years in too much space –
that's the thing that's hard to face,
and . . .

You have a right to go,
but you should also know
that I won't be alone for long.
Long days with nothing said
are not what lie ahead –
I'm sorry but I'm not that strong.

Anything but lonely,
anything but passing time.
Lonely's what I'll never be,
while there's still some life in me,
and . . .

I'm still young, don't forget,
it isn't over yet –
so many hearts for me to thrill.
If you're not here to say
how good I look each day,
I'll have to find someone who will . . .

Anything but lonely,
anything but empty rooms.
There's so much in life to share –
what's the sense when no-one else is there?

Love Changes Everything

Music by Andrew Lloyd Webber
Lyrics by Don Black & Charles Hart

15

sum - mer fly / or a night / seem like / a life - time. / Yes
world a - round / and that world / will last / for ev - er. / Yes

love, / love chan - ges / ev - ery - thing: / now I trem - ble / at your
love, / love chan - ges / ev - ery - thing, / brings you glo - ry, / brings you

name. / No - thing in the world will ev - er / be / the
shame. / No - thing in the world will ev - er / be / the

cresc.

1.
same.

2.
same. _____

f

cresc.

Off _____ in - to the world we go, plan-ning fu - tures, shap-ing years.

Love _____ bursts in and sud-den-ly, all our wis - dom dis - ap - pears.

Love _____ makes fools of ev - ery-one: all the rules we make are

PARLEZ-VOUS FRANÇAIS?

Music by Andrew Lloyd Webber
Lyrics by Don Black & Charles Hart

SEEING IS BELIEVING

Music by Andrew Lloyd Webber
Lyrics by Don Black & Charles Hart

night we'll mean the things we say for - ev - - - er. See-ing is be -

liev - ing! My life is just be - gin - ning! We touched, and my head won't stop

spin - ning _____ from win - ning _____ your love! _____

Chanson D'Enfance

Music by Andrew Lloyd Webber
Lyrics by Don Black & Charles Hart

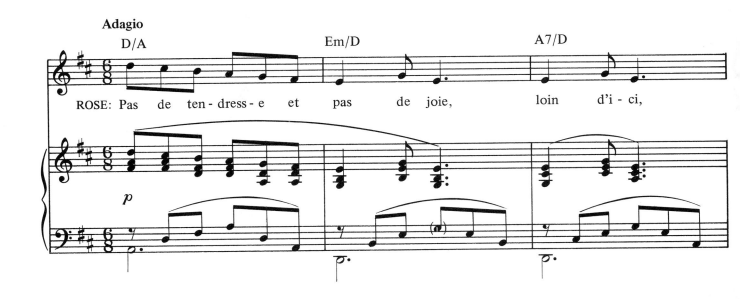

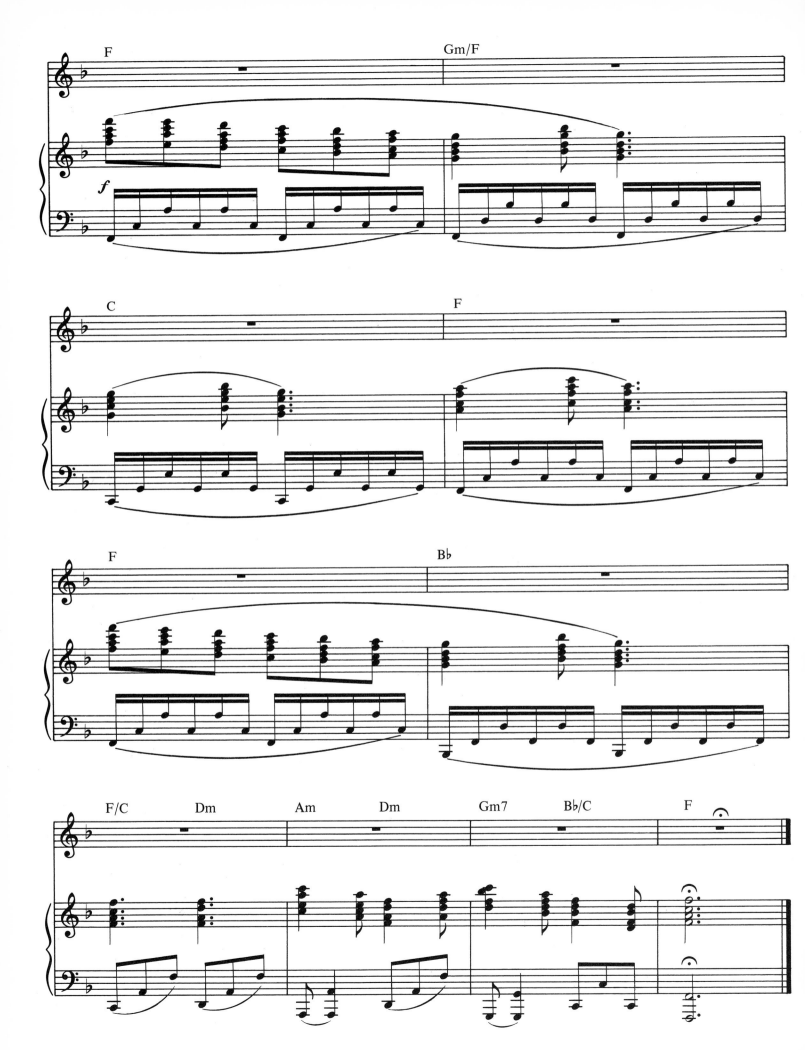

OTHER PLEASURES

Music by Andrew Lloyd Webber
Lyrics by Don Black & Charles Hart

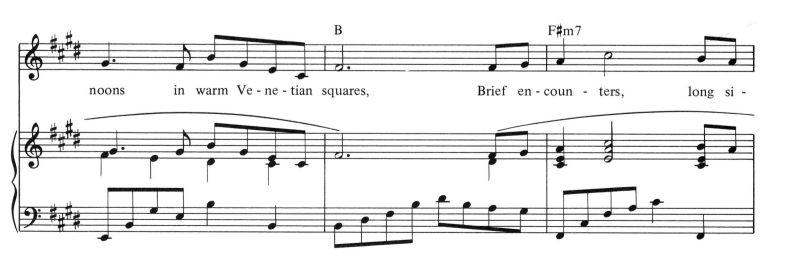

MERMAID SONG

Music by Andrew Lloyd Webber
Lyrics by Don Black & Charles Hart

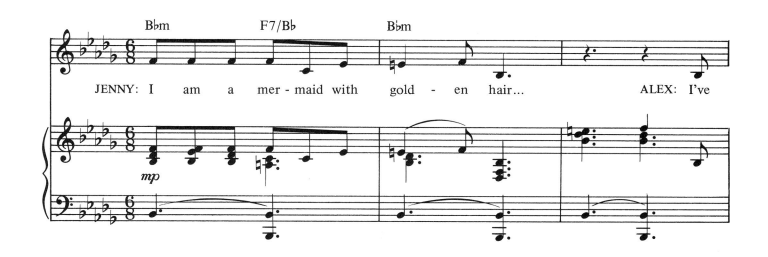

JENNY: I am a mer - maid with gold - en hair... ALEX: I've

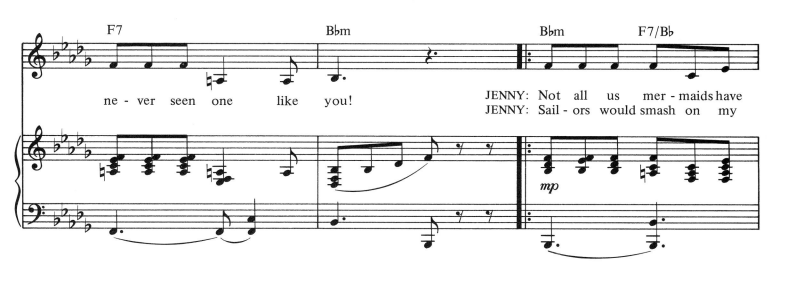

ne - ver seen one like you!

JENNY: Not all us mer - maids have
JENNY: Sail - ors would smash on my

sil - ver tails— I have no tail at all. ALEX: Well I've ne - ver
jag - ged rock, lured by my si - ren's song. ALEX: It is - n't the

35

seen an - y mer-maids with knob - bly knees!
song of the si - ren that tor - tures men—

I'd say this tale was a
that's where your theo - ry goes

touch too tall,
sad - ly wrong,

may - be a touch too tall. _____
that's where it all goes wrong. _____

JENNY: I thought you'd know bet - ter. ___ You know no - thing ___ a - bout

mer - maids. ___ You know no - thing ___ a - bout sail - ors. ___ JENNY: I

ALEX:

THE FIRST MAN YOU REMEMBER

Music by Andrew Lloyd Webber
Lyrics by Don Black & Charles Hart

GEORGE: I want to be the first man you re-

mem - ber, I want to be the last man you'll for-

floor? The ve - ry first to see your face by

moon - light? The ve - ry first to walk you to your

door? JENNY: Well young man I'll be de - light - ed! _____

_____ There is no - thing I would ra - ther

feet;   GEORGE: I want to be the one you al - ways

turn to... _____ The first to walk my young heart miss a

beat.

GEORGE: Seems the

stars are far be - low us ___ us ___

The moon has ne-ver felt like this be-fore

BOTH: our first dance will be for-

ev - er. And may it lead to ma-ny more. I

want to be the first man you re-mem - ber ...

HAND ME THE WINE AND THE DICE

Music by Andrew Lloyd Webber
Lyrics by Don Black & Charles Hart

GIULIETTA:
George was an o - ri - gi - nal man. ___ He did

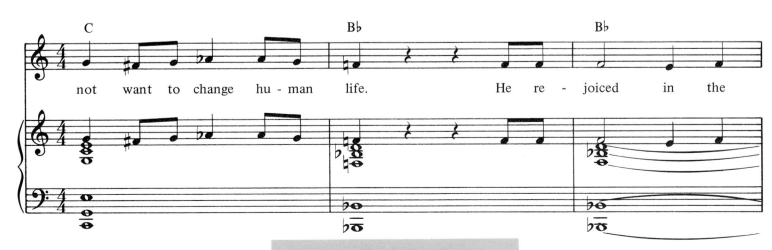

not want to change hu - man life. He re - joiced in the

way we are made.__ He did not look for - ward to hea - ven— he was

hap - py with the earth. He loved and un - der-stood the flesh, food, wine, love...

He lived for to - day _____ and firm - ly be - lieved:

If death were gi - ven a voice, __ that voice would

scream through the sky:___   live while you may, for I am

com - ing... ___   So...   Hand me the
Hand me the

wine and the dice, ___   I want my car - ni - val now, ___
wine and the dice, ___   the time is rac - ing a - way—___

while I have thirst and lust for liv - ing! ___
there's not a taste that's not worth try - ing! ___

48

So ga-ther all you can reap, __
And if, to - mor-row it ends, __

be-fore you're un-der the plough— __   the hand of
I won't have wast-ed to - day— __   I will have

To Coda ⊕

death is un - for - giv - ing! __
lived when I am dy - ing! __

Hand me the wine and the dice, __   while there are

grapes on the vine—___   life is a round of end - less

plea - sures!_____   The end is

al - ways in sight,___   but it tastes bet - ter with wine—

why pour your life in ti - ny mea - sures?_____

ALEX: *(Spoken)* George always said, people can have more than one emotion at the same time. One makes the other even more acute, then cures it.

CHORUS

Hand me the wine and the dice,___ while there are

grapes on the vine— life is a round of end - less

plea - sures! The end is

al -ways in sight, ___ but it tastes bet - ter with wine—

why. pour your life in ti - ny mea - sures? ___

death is un - for - giv - ing. _____

GIULIETTA: You must be the fa - mous A - lex!   ALEX: You must be Giu - li - et - ta!

GIULIETTA: Tell me, are you still shoot - ing wo - men?

(CHORUS) (Hand me the

ALEX: Rose ne - ver could keep a se - cret.

wine and the dice —)

GIULIETTA: Rose and I hide no-thing.

ALEX: I heard you got on well to-ge - ther.

GIULIETTA: *(Spoken)* Death says: live while you may, for I am coming.

Do you dance with women of your *own* age?

lived when I am dy - ing! _____

Hand me the wine and the dice, ___ I want my car - ni - val now, ___ while I have thirst and lust for

Anything But Lonely

Music by Andrew Lloyd Webber
Lyrics by Don Black & Charles Hart

what's the sense when no - one else is there?
that's the thing that's hard to face, and...

You have a right to go, but you should al - so know that I won't be a - lone for long.

Long days with no - thing said are not what lie a - head— I'm sor - ry but I'm not that strong.

A - ny - thing but lone - ly, a - ny - thing but

pass-ing time.   Lone-ly's what I'll   ne - ver be,   while there's still some

life   in   me,   and...   I'm still young, don't for-get,   it is - n't ov - er yet—

so ma - ny hearts for me to   thrill.   If   you're not here to say

how good I   look each day,   I'll have to   find some-one who   will...

A - ny-thing but lone - ly, a - ny-thing but emp-ty rooms.

There's so much in life to share— what's the sense when no - one else is

there? What's the sense when

no one else is there? _____

ADDITIONAL SONGS

She'd Be Far Better Off With You

Music by Andrew Lloyd Webber
Lyrics by Don Black & Charles Hart

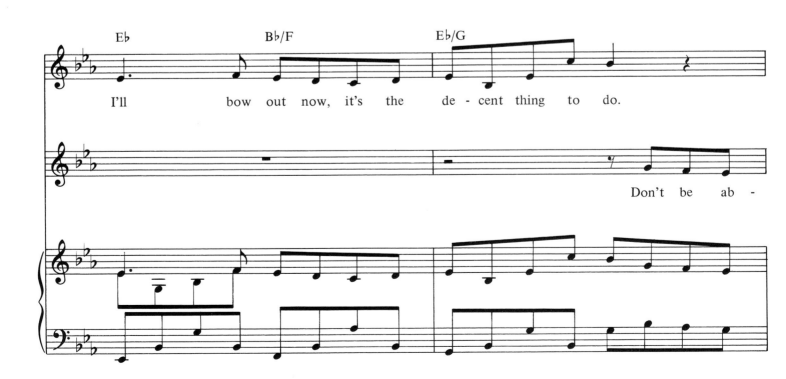

I'm a dis-as-ter.   It would-n't last a week.   She'd be far bet-ter off with

-surd.   Oh come, come.

you.   It would end in mur-der.   I'm   too old for her. It's

You   two have your lives be - fore   you.

Your place   is   here.   It's the

high time   I   with - drew.   The jowls   are   drop - ping.

las un-true. It's on-ly Rose that mat-ters! Just take a

las un-true. It's on-ly Rose that mat-ters! Just take a

look, there's no com-pa-ri-son be-tween us two.

look, there's no com-pa-ri-son be-tween us two.

She'd be far bet-ter off with you.

She'd be far bet-ter off with you.

THERE IS MORE TO LOVE

Music by Andrew Lloyd Webber
Lyrics by Don Black & Charles Hart

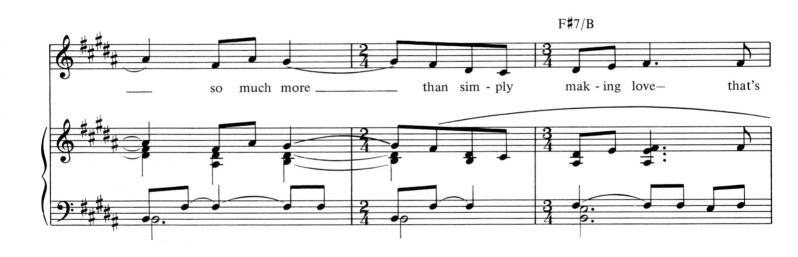

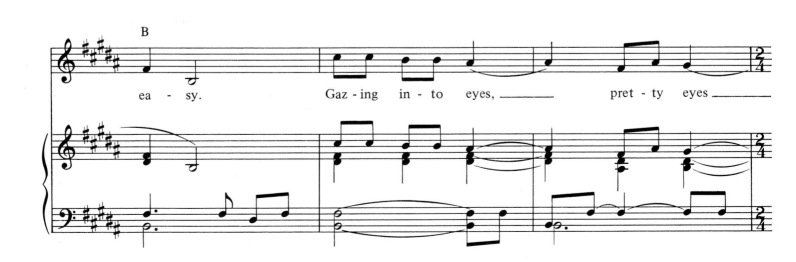

Now each time love rea - ches out to me, I can on - ly feel ___ there has to be so much more to love.

There is more to love, ___ so much more.